Dedication

To Mom, Dad, Aleya, Zane and Grandma — for the unconditional love and support.

And to Nora and Jordan — for making my Georgetown experience what it was and for being by my side every single step of the way.

Contents

1. *Getting There*
   From home to the Hilltop

2. *Your Studies*
   Tips to acing college learning

3. *The Mall*
   The Heart of D.C.

4. *All things Georgetown*
   Need-to-know Georgetown facts

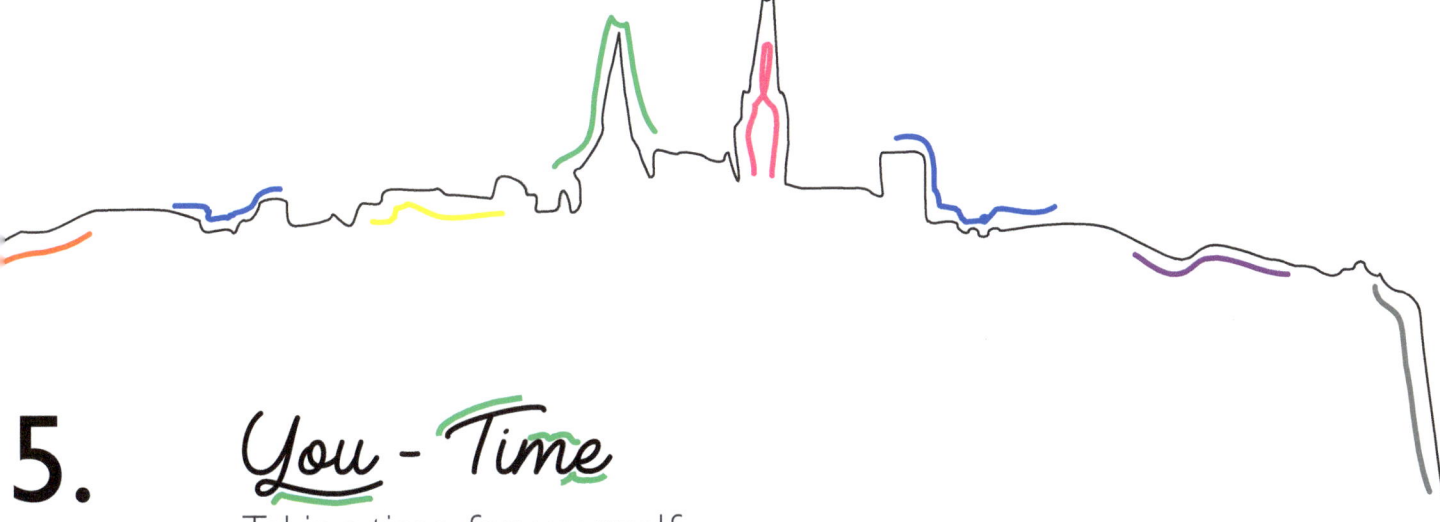

5. *You - Time*
Taking time for yourself

6. *Eats*
My favorite places to eat in D.C.

7. *Georgetown Traditions*
Georgetown's most important traditions

8. *Conclusion*
Closing remarks and the best advice I can give

1. Getting There
From home to the Hilltop

1. Let yourself be excited. You are entering a new chapter of your life, one that may define aspects of your career, character, and values for the next four years and one that will bring lots and lots of fun times. It's okay to get stoked.

2. Leave your expectations at home. While you should not control your level of excitement, do restrict yourself from setting your mind on exactly what you expect to encounter when you first get to Georgetown.

3. Keep an open mind – to everything. Let yourself get swept up trying new things and meeting new people. Do not be scared to introduce yourself.

4. Know that you will miss home. It may take you one hour, one month, or one year, but be prepared to feel homesick, no matter how excited you may be.

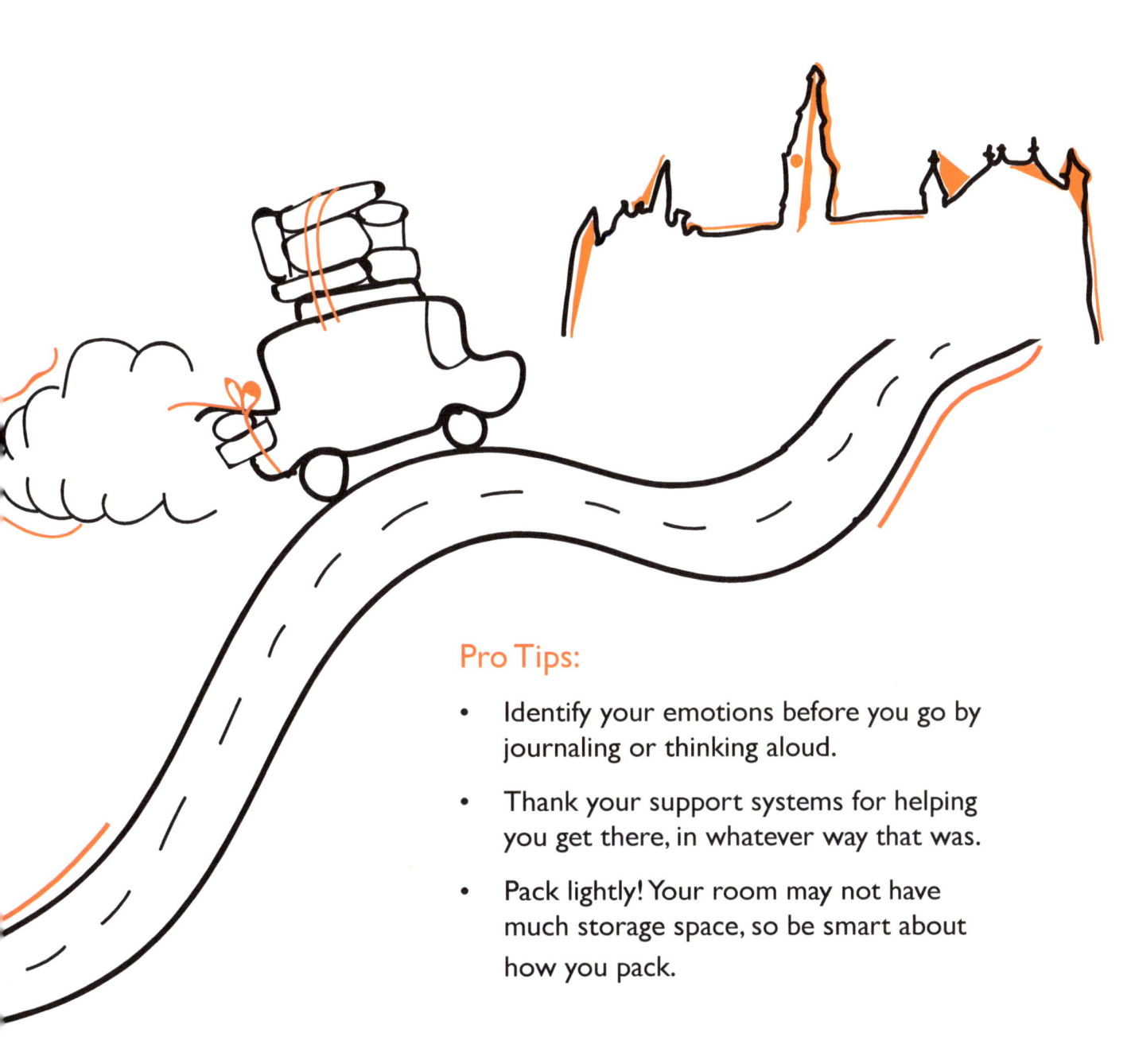

Pro Tips:

- Identify your emotions before you go by journaling or thinking aloud.
- Thank your support systems for helping you get there, in whatever way that was.
- Pack lightly! Your room may not have much storage space, so be smart about how you pack.

2. Your Studies

Tips to acing college learning

Get to know your professors

Introduce yourself on the first day and never shy away from reaching out. Later in the semester, if you're doing well, your professor can match your face to your work. Conversely, if you're struggling, they will be more inclined to give you a break if they recognize you or you have a personal relationship.

Get Organized

Having a planner or calendar will help you keep track of your assignments and their due dates. You would be surprised how often you can forget a night's homework if you don't write it down!

Read Before Class

Reading is not real homework, right? Wrong. Okay…well technically you could get away without it. And so many times, I did. However, on the days I really prepared, I was able to fully engage and got much more out of the class. My professors noticed a change, I looked forward to going to class more and I was able to finish my assignments much quicker.

Know Your Peers

Your fellow classmates are invaluable assets to your college education. Studying with others who have different educational backgrounds, methods of study and personalities will offer you perspectives on the material that you won't get from studying on your own. Find some peers to study with you and organize study groups with them. If you can't find anyone, reach out to your professor and I guarantee he or she will help you find someone!

Find Your Spot

Find a spot, on campus or otherwise, where you know you can really get into your study zone. When you have something important due, go straight there! Don't waste time looking for new spots when the clock is ticking. When you don't have an impending deadline, explore away! There are lots of nice coffee shops in the area.

Take Breaks

It is proven that our brains do not function well when we try to work for hours on end. To avoid wasting precious study time, take intentional breaks. Some good methods that I know are to work for 45 minutes and take 15 minutes off or work for 25 minutes and take 5 minutes off.

3. The Mall

The Heart of D.C.

Washington, D.C. is an amazing city full of history. You should never forget that the National Mall is in your backyard. Here's what you should see when you go.

Monuments

- Korean War Veterans Memorial
- Thomas Jefferson Memorial
- Vietnam Veterans Memorial
- Martin Luther King, Jr. Memorial
- World War II Memorial
- Washington Monument
- Lincoln Memorial
- Friendship Archway

Check them out at night too. The building lights go on and they look even bigger!

Museums

- National Air and Space Museum
- National Archives
- Newseum
- National Museum of the American Indian
- National Building Museum
- National Museum of Natural History
- Smithsonian American Art Museum
- International Spy Museum

Galleries

- The National Gallery of Art (East Gallery)
  Constitution Ave. between Third and Seventh Sts., NW, Free

- The Renwick Gallery
  1661 Pennsylvania Ave., NW, Free

- The National Portrait Gallery
  Eighth and F Sts., NW, Free

- The National Museum of Women in the Arts
  1250 New York Ave., NW, $8 – $10

- Hirschorn Museum and Sculpture Garden
  7 St. and Independence Ave., SW, Free

- The National Museum of African Art
  950 Independence Ave., SW, Free

- The Phillips Collection
  1600 21st St., NW, $10 – $12

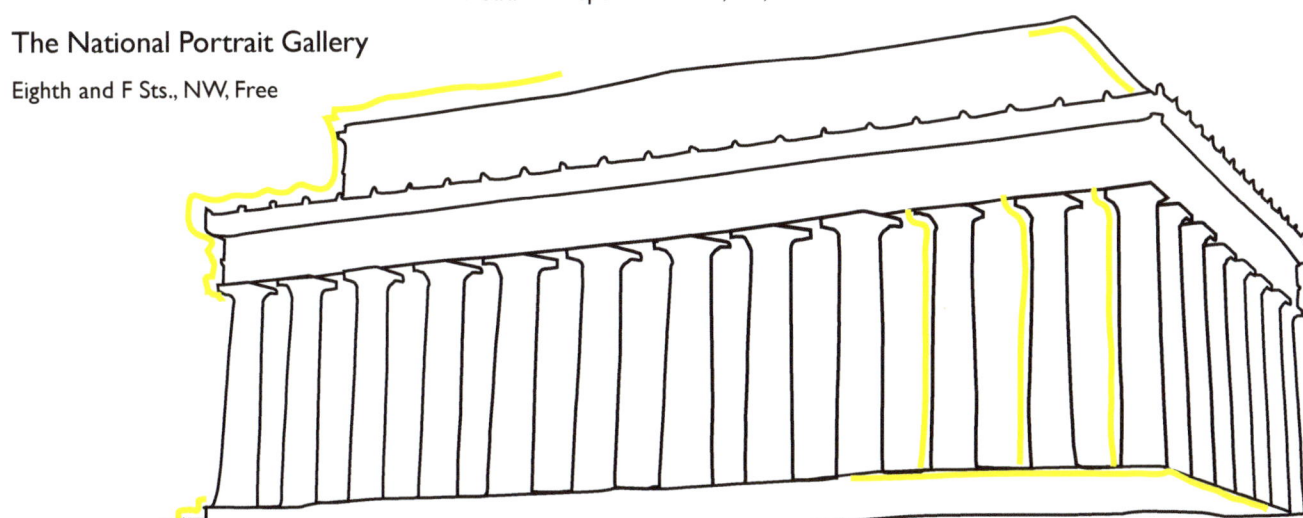

4. All things Georgetown

If you're on your way to Georgetown you've surely heard the saying "Hoya Saxa." The phrase comes from an old chant saying "What Rocks" using Greek and Latin terms, referring to the football team who were nicknamed the "stonewalls." Now, we yell it at sporting games or any events to show pride. The term "Hoyas" stuck so we call ourselves the Georgetown Hoyas although it isn't our official mascot. You'll hear plenty of variations of the phrase such as "Hoya Snaxa" a convenience store on campus, or "The Hoya" a Georgetown newspaper.

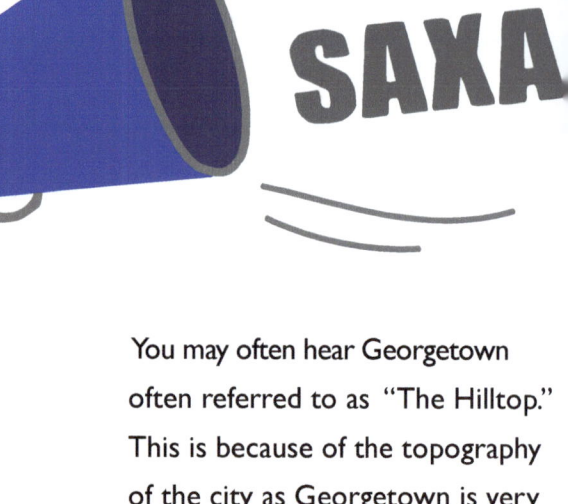

The Hilltop

You may often hear Georgetown often referred to as "The Hilltop." This is because of the topography of the city as Georgetown is very much situated on a hill. For this reason, the campus is covered in stairs and you'll find yourself ascending and descending quite a bit. Get ready for toned calves!

Jack the Bulldog

Our real mascot at Georgetown is a bulldog. Although we often call ourselves the Hoyas, the bulldog is our animal representation. We have a real bulldog, a bit like a school pet, named Jack the Bulldog. There have been lots of Jacks throughout the years. Each one is trained rigorously, mainly to stand around and look cute in front of people. You'll see him at big events on campus, or taking a walk with his owner, a Jesuit resident. If you want to be part of Jack's life, apply to be a walker! Students take shifts walking him around campus and through the neighborhood.

12
1
2
3
4
6
7
8
9
10
11

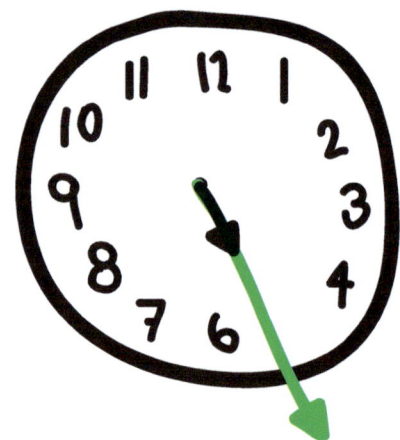

Taking time for yourself

Being a college student has its ups and downs. While it is can be fun and exciting, it can also be stressful and overwhelming at times. You must remember to take care of your mental, emotional and physical health. On the next page are a few ways I kept these aspects in check and why I think it is so important to do so.

5. You-Time

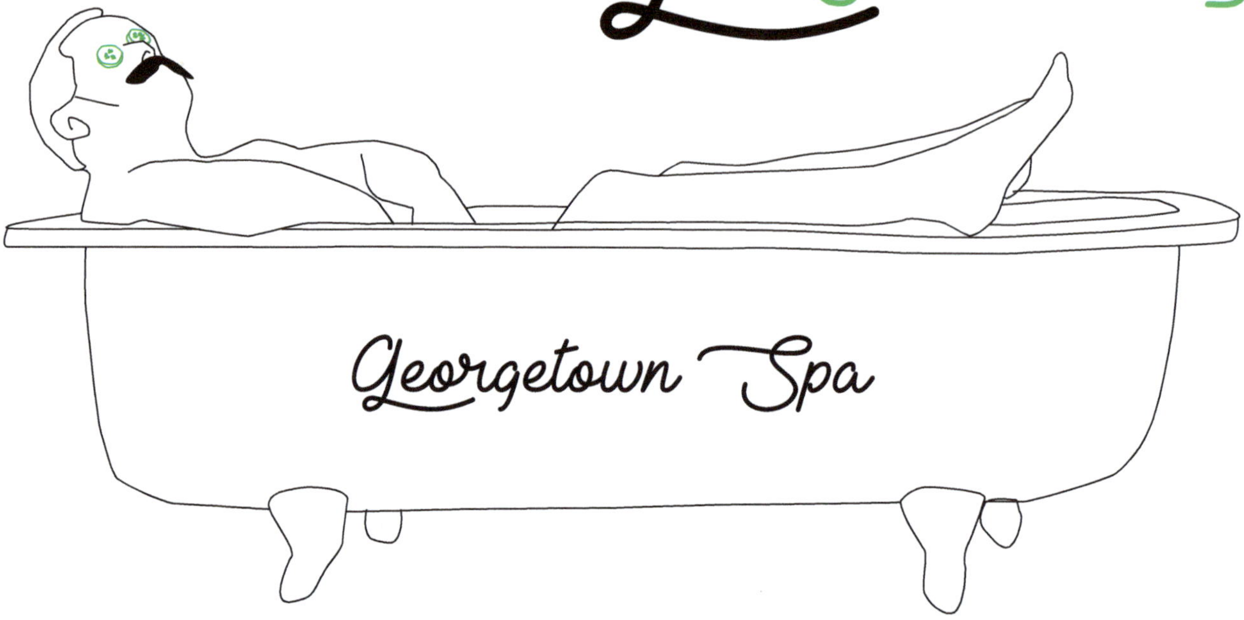
Georgetown Spa

Get Rest

Sleep is an essential part of our lives. In college especially, when you may be overwhelmed by the various sectors of your life, it is so important to let your body rest. Although the ideal 8–9 hours is often unrealistic as a student, do not settle for less than 6–7. If you get behind on a night or two, consider skipping a night out to catch up.

Eat Well

Your diet affects the way you feel, sleep and your energy throughout the day. Load up on grains, proteins, vegetables and fruits. Try to avoid too much sugar, caffeine and fats that will keep you up at night or bog you down during the day. There's no need to cut anything out completely, just strive for balance.

Get exercise

Regardless of your athletic background, I encourage you to make exercise a part of your weekly routine. The rush of endorphins is destressing and will help you to balance your days. Yates, the gym is a great start. If you like classes, check out SoulCycle for cycling or CorePower Yoga for yoga. If you like being outdoors, as I do, there are lots of beautiful paths such as the Towpath lining the C+O canal, Rock Creek Park, or the river path to the monuments.

Get out

You will be working very hard while being a student. You can't forget to take some nights off to go out and let loose. You'll encounter many different events on campus and once you turn 21, D.C. has a ton of cool bars and clubs.

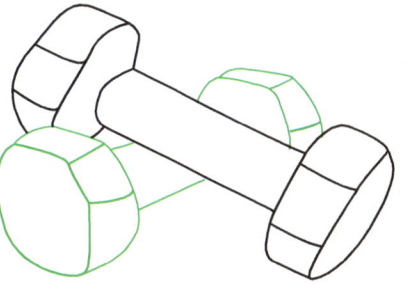

6.

Eats

Georgetown and the greater D.C. area have tons of great food. Below, listed, in no particular order, are some of my favorites spots along with my favorite things to get there.

Ted's Bulletin is an old-fashioned style diner on 14th st. Everything on the menu is delicious, but I get the French Toast every time because it comes with hash browns and eggs and I love the sweet and savory mix. Hit their bakery before you leave to try their famous Pop-tarts. They are a unique homemade treat—the salted caramel flavor is truly spectacular.

Momofuku CCDC is a truly unique cuisine experience. New to the D.C. scene but established in N.Y.C., they have an innovative take on all foods. Try their pork buns or ramen for lunch or dinner and their Cake Truffles for dessert.

Lincoln Restaurant is known for its seasonal small plates and Abraham Lincoln themed decor. I recommend the Lincoln Kale Salad, the Mac n' Cheese and the risotto.

Surfside is a Mexican style restaurant with locations in Georgetown and Dupont Circle. The Steak Quesadilla is a special treat and their buttery yellow rice is to-die-for. When the weather gets nice, visit the Georgetown location and enjoy a meal or a drink on their colorful and beautifully decorated rooftop.

South Block is a delicious and healthy smoothie, juice and small bite shop. Their Acai bowls are incredibly tasty and very filling and their caveman mylk is a delicious and refreshing dairy alternative. If you make it to their Clarendon location, the Elvis wrap is a must-try!

Farmers Fishers Bakers is an upscale casual restaurant on the waterfront. It is supplied by farmers across the country and the difference in freshness is easy to notice. My favorite part about this restaurant is called First Bake. On weekdays from 8:30 – 11:00 am, they offer delicious breakfast treats at crazy low prices—not to mention with a view!

Pizzeria Paradiso is an authentic Pizzeria with fluffy pizza crust and an incredible mix of flavors. Both the Georgetown and Dupont spots have relaxed ambiances that will make you want to stay all day eating pizza. Don't leave without trying the Bianca!

Rasika is one of D.C.'s most famous restaurants and lives up to its reputation. It offers small plates, taking a modern spin on and old approach to dining. Rasika means flavors in sanskrit, and trying anything on the menu will convince you of it.

Desserts

If you haven't heard, Georgetown has a bit of a cupcake rivalry. Here are the top spots along with my favorite flavors.

- **Sprinkles** – Chocolate, Red Velvet (if you like cream cheese frosting!)

- **Georgetown Cupcake** – Vanilla^2, Salted Caramel, Chocolate Peppermint

- **Baked and Wired** – (called cakecups there) Strawberry, Vegan Oreo, Pumpkin

- If you are more of an ice cream person, **Thomas Sweet** is by far the best in town.

7. Georgetown Traditions

Sit on John Carroll's Lap

Bishop John Carroll, the founder of Georgetown, has a statue of himself seated right in front of the iconic Healy hall. It is a Georgetown tradition to sit on the statue's lap before you graduate. It's a bit of a ways off the ground, so bring a friend to give you a boost!

JOHN CARROLL
FOVNDER

Get your forehead stamped at The Tombs

Possibly the most important tradition to follow is spending your 21st birthday at The Tombs. At midnight the night you turn 21, go to the tombs with friends and have them stamp your forehead instead of your hand so everyone knows its your birthday.

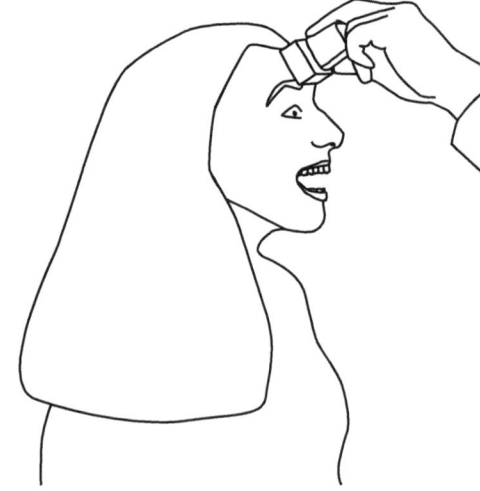

See the cherry blossoms at the tidal basin

Usually from the end of March to the beginning of April, these beautiful Japanese flowers bloom and surround the entire area with pink and white pedals. The thousands of trees were a peace offering from the Japanese to the Americans at the end of World War II. The Cherry Blossoms in the south of Japan bloom at the same time, so we still share that bond as we admire the flowers yearly.

Do not step on the seal

It is said that if you step on the seal that blocks the pathway into Healy hall, you will be cursed and will not graduate from Georgetown. This myth is so strictly followed that the seal is breaking in half from students walking around it and putting all the weight on the sides. The day you graduate, feel free to stomp all over it.

8. Before you go...

College will be a special time in your life. You will learn a lot – in an educational sense as well as a personal one. You will meet new people every day and create meaningful connections with those who you share interests with. You will leave Georgetown with skills that you did not have before entering and you will be an expert in the field of study that you chose. You will make friends that influence you in positive ways and who you will never forget.

However, it won't be a breeze. You will be working very hard to stay on top of your classes, you may have trouble finding people who share your interests, you may not know which major suits you best, you may be upset with your living situation, etc. I say this not to put a damper on your excitement, but to prepare you in the best way I can.

My first semester at Georgetown came with a whirlwind of emotions and experiences. I had many good times, and some not so good ones. I remember thinking that semester "Why didn't anyone tell me college was hard? I thought it was only fun." So, as my gift to you, I am giving you a warning. I want you to know what's in store. And, now that you know this, you have about 15 pages on all of my favorite things to do in Georgetown. I would have *killed* to have better known what to do with my time here, and looking back, I wish I could have done all these things 10 times more often than I did. In case you skimmed over the past few pages, this last page holds the most valuable takeaways from my four years here. I hope you enjoyed the book, and have a spectacular time at Georgetown.

Don't let your studies consume you

Many Georgetown students get caught up with their work and forget that life exists outside of the library. I promise you will regret four years spent only doing work. Do your best in all of your classes, and by all means delve into your interests. But do not forget to leave your work for a few nights a week to spend time with friend, explore the city, or attend a speaker on campus. Making human connections and experiencing a new city are two of the most important take aways from college. Don't let them slip away.

Get to know your professors

Georgetown professors can be truly invaluable connections. If they have been hired to teach you a given subject, they are often elite in that field. If you liked a certain professor, stay in touch with them. Ask them to coffee one day to learn more about what they do or the road that led them to Georgetown. They might inspire you to pursue a career path, or even connect you to peers that may offer you a job later down the line.

Don't be afraid to be yourself

Coming from high school, we feel that our identities are fixed. Georgetown is a perfect place to question this. If something interests you, test it out and see if it sticks. You may surprised by liking something you previously thought you never would.

Join clubs

Georgetown students tend to form social groups around the clubs they are in. So join more than you think you want to be in, and later leave if you aren't interested or you don't click with the other members.

Reflect

Reflect a lot and reflect often. So much will happen in your four years here. You will leave a different person than you came in. To understand the changes going on, question yourself about the impact that your experiences are having on you. When you're happy with something, ask yourself why. When you're not happy with something, know why too. Take note of your answers, and during your time here you will get to know yourself quite well.

This book was written by me, **Camilla Spielman**, during March and April of my senior year. Leading up to graduation, I found myself thinking a lot about my time at Georgetown. I thought about the good times, all the things I learned, and all the things I would have done differently. The biggest thing I realized was that I knew very little about what to expect at Georgetown before getting here. This short book is a condensed summary of all the tips I have. From advice on school work to my favorite restaurants in the area, I hope this survival guide will point you in the right direction in many different parts of your life. I learned much of it the hard way and I learned much of it too late, so this is my attempt at giving you the tools to have the best Georgetown experience possible.

Best of luck!

www.ingramcontent.com/pod-product-compliance
Lightning Source LLC
Chambersburg PA
CBHW041408160426
42811CB00103B/1555